Julia Barnes

GARETH**STEVENS**
PUBLISHING
A Member of the WRC Media Family of Companies

Please visit our web site at: www.garethstevens.com
For a free color catalog describing Gareth Stevens Publishing's
list of high-quality books and multimedia programs, call
1-800-542-2595 (USA) or 1-800-387-3178 (Canada).
Gareth Stevens Publishing's fax: (414) 332-3567.

Library of Congress Cataloging-in-Publication Data

Barnes, Julia, 1955-
  Pet parakeets / Julia Barnes. — North American ed.
   p. cm. — (Pet pals)
  Includes bibliographical references and index.
  ISBN-10: 0-8368-6780-7 — ISBN-13: 978-0-8368-6780-0 (lib. bdg.)
  1. Parrots—Juvenile literature. I. Title.
  SF473.P3B37   2007
  636.6'865—dc22   2006042375

This edition first published in 2007 by
Gareth Stevens Publishing
A Member of the WRC Media Family of Companies
330 West Olive Street, Suite 100
Milwaukee, Wisconsin 53212 USA

This U.S. edition copyright © 2007 by Gareth Stevens, Inc.
Original edition copyright © 2006 by Westline Publishing,
P.O. Box 8, Lydney, Gloucestershire, GL15 6YD, United Kingdom.

Gareth Stevens series editor: Leifa Butrick
Gareth Stevens cover design: Dave Kowalski
Gareth Stevens art direction: Tammy West

Picture Credits:
Oxford Scientific, pp. 4 (Konrad Wothe), 6 (Roger Brown); Bonnie Jacobs
(iStockphoto.com), p. 8; Warren Photographic, pp. 9, 21 (Jane Burton).
All other images copyright © 2006 by Westline Publishing.

Printed in the United States of America

1 2 3 4 5 6 7 8 9 10 09 08 07 06

Cover: A parakeet often feeds its companion
as a special sign of affection.

Contents

Words that appear in the glossary are printed in
boldface type the first time they occur in the text.

In the Wild

Parakeets are members of the parrot family, a very colorful group of birds.

More than three hundred types of parrots live in Africa, Asia, North and South America, and Australia. The parakeet that we know as a pet comes from central Australia. Huge **flocks** of parakeets, often with tens of thousands of birds, fly over Australian grasslands.

On the Wing

Wild parakeets eat grasses and grass seeds, eucalyptus leaves, berries, and sometimes insects. In the dry conditions of the Australian **outback**, parakeets are always moving from place to place, looking for water and fresh food supplies.

Wild parakeets fly together in huge flocks.

This parakeet has found a hollow, high in the treetops, to use as a nest.

The only time parakeets stop traveling is when rainfall has made many plants grow and there is plenty of food. Then they stop to breed. Parakeets do not build nests of sticks, however. They lay their eggs and raise their **chicks** in the hollows of trees. Because the whole flock breeds at the same time, all the chicks are ready to **fledge**, or leave the nest, at the same time. Then the flock flies off again.

What's in a Name?

In the United States, a parakeet, or "keet," is a small bird from Australia that is kept as a pet. In the United Kingdom, the same bird is known as a budgerigar, or "budgie."

Plain and Simple

Compared to many unusual members of the parrot family, wild parakeets are not flashy-looking birds. They are green with yellow faces, and they have black markings on their wings. All wild parakeets have the same coloring, and they are smaller and thinner than pet parakeets.

Breeders today have produced parakeets in a dazzling range of colors, and their birds are still hardy and easy to care for.

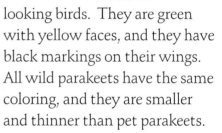

Keet Care

In the wild, snakes and hawks hunt parakeets, but the greatest danger parakeets face is extreme **drought** conditions. Adult birds die from lack of water. If there is a water shortage when the birds are breeding, many chicks die before they ever leave their nests.

The Human Link

Americans and Europeans first found out about parakeets after Captain James Cook explored Australia in 1770.

British sailors who had been to Australia told stories about pretty green birds that flew in such large flocks that they blotted out the Sun. When the birds landed on the branches of a dead tree, their brilliant green **plumage** made the tree look as if it had come back to life.

When early settlers in Australia met the native **Aborigines**, the settlers asked what the birds were called. The Aborigines' answer sounded like "betchery-gah" so the settlers named the birds "budgerigars." Later, when the Aboriginal word was translated, Westerners discovered that the word meant "good to eat."

In the wild, a mother parakeet feeds her chick by giving it food from her beak. Adult parakeets also feed one another as a sign of affection.

Parakeets have been able to adapt from a life in the wild to living in cages.

New Breeds

English explorer and **naturalist** John Gould returned from a trip to Australia in 1840 and brought a pair of parakeets back to England with him. The plain-looking, green birds, which were about 4 inches (10 centimeters) long, interested breeders. The first pure yellow parakeet, bred in Belgium in 1870, caused a sensation. After that, breeders became more and more competitive, in their attempts to produce new colors and new varieties of parakeets.

Royal Connections

The first sky-blue parakeets were bred in England in 1910. Members of the Japanese royal family were so impressed they paid a huge amount of money to import a pair of blue parakeets for their own breeding program. Soon, Japanese nobility started a custom of giving blue parakeets as love tokens.

At first, only wealthy people owned parakeets, but as the birds became more common, all kinds of people adopted them as pets. When Europeans emigrated to the United States, in the early part of the twentieth century, some took their favorite pets with them, including, of course, parakeets.

Did You Know?

In the early days of keeping parakeets, people caught birds in the wild by spreading huge nets over the birds' favorite feeding areas. When pet parakeets started breeding, there was no longer a need to catch wild birds.

Perfect Pets

Today, parakeets are the most popular of all pet birds.

- Parakeets are hardy birds, and, with the right care, they develop few health problems.
- Parakeets are small in size and do not need as much living space as parrots.
- Parakeets get along well with each other and can live in pairs or in small groups.
- Parakeets are great **mimics** and can even learn to talk.
- Parakeets can live for seven or eight years.

- Parakeets like people and will bond closely with their owners.

A Parakeet's Needs

A parakeet is an easy bird to keep as a pet, but it has certain needs that owners should know about. In the past, keeping a bird in a cage twenty-four hours a day was considered all right. Now we realize that this is an unkind way to keep a pet bird.

A parakeet is easy to look after and fun to be with.

8

Parakeet breeders often keep their birds in **aviaries**, where the birds have space to fly. Most parakeet owners keep their parakeets in cages, but they must take extra care to meet special needs of caged birds.

All parakeets need the freedom to fly for awhile each day.

- Bird cages need to be cleaned every day.
- Caged birds must be allowed out of their cages for at least an hour every day so they can fly. Owners need to provide a safe, secure area where their birds can fly but cannot escape.
- A parakeet without a companion will become bored and lonely. People who want pet parakeets need to keep at least two birds so they are company for each other.
- When owners must be away from home for more than a day, they need to find someone to look after their parakeets.

Allergy Alert

If you have an **allergy** to pets with fur – causing health problems such as breathing difficulties, itchy skin, or watery eyes – you will probably find that parakeets will not give you such problems.

A Parakeet's Body

A parakeet's body allows it to fly and to climb easily.

Nose
A parakeet's nose is located just above its upper beak. No feathers cover this area of its face. The waxy skin there is known as the **cere**. Male parakeets, called **cocks**, have blue ceres. Females, called **hens**, have brown ceres.

Beak
A parakeet's curved beak is perfect for cracking open seeds. Parakeets also use their beaks for climbing and for **preening**.

Feathers
Short **contour feathers** cover a parakeet's body.

Body
A parakeet has a **streamlined** body. Its sleek shape is essential for flight.

Toes
A parakeet has two pairs of toes. One pair points forward. The other pair points backward. A parakeet uses its toes to climb.

Keet Care
Parakeets have body temperatures of 104 to 108° Fahrenheit (40 to 42° Celsius). A parakeet will fluff out its feathers to keep warm and will pant when it needs to cool down.

Ears

A parakeet's ears are hidden beneath its feathers on either side of its head. When a parakeet is wet after taking a bath, its small ear holes can be seen. Compared to people, parakeets have poor hearing.

Eyes

Three eyelids protect a parakeet's eyes. Besides an upper and a lower, a third eyelid covers the surface of the eyeball. A parakeet can see to the sides as well as to the front.

Wings

A parakeet's wings have long **flight feathers** that create a large wingspan, which is necessary for flight.

Rump

A parakeet has a gland on its lower back that produces an oily substance that the bird uses to protect its feathers from dust and water. A parakeet spreads the oil over its feathers when the bird is preening.

Vent

A bird's body has an opening, called a vent, that is used for breeding and for getting rid of waste.

Tail

A parakeet's tail is made up of long feathers to help the bird balance during flight.

Parakeet Colors

Parakeet breeders have created more than one hundred different colors of pet parakeets.

This yellow parakeet has red eyes.

The first pet parakeets were easy to breed. Soon, there was no need to go to Australia to get parakeets from the wild. Then breeders produced a yellow parakeet, followed by sky-blue parakeets. People came to realize that by breeding birds of different colors, they could invent many new colors. Now, we have a fantastic variety to choose from.

Green
Parakeets come in light green, dark green, and olive green.

Green parakeets have yellow faces and green bodies.

Blue
Blue parakeets also come in several shades. The darkest is sky blue, the next is cobalt blue, and the lightest shade is mauve, which is a light purple.

Lutino

Pure yellow parakeets are called lutinos. They have no other colors in their plumage.

Albino

Parakeets with no coloring are white, or albino, and they have red eyes.

Cinnamon

Cinnamon parakeets are light brown. The wings of a cinnamon parakeet have black and brown stripes.

Diluted

Pale-colored feathers are sometimes called diluted.

Gray

Some parakeets are gray: light gray, medium gray, or dark gray.

Clearwing

A clearwing parakeet is very attractive. It may have a blue body with white wings or a green body with yellow wings.

Crested or Tufted

Crested and tufted parakeets are unusual looking.

A pied parakeet has patches of white in its blue plumage.

A crested parakeet has a fringe of feathers that circles its head. The tufted variety has a crest of feathers that sticks up at the front of its head.

Keet Homes

Parakeets need housing that is large enough for them to fly around in.

Parakeet breeders keep their birds in aviaries, which is an ideal arrangement. The parakeets have freedom to fly, and they can enjoy the company of other birds. Aviaries vary in design. They usually have a large outside flight area and an inside sleeping compartment. The flight area is usually fenced in with wire netting.

Cages

If you plan to keep parakeets in a cage, buy the biggest cage you can afford. The birds' flying muscles need exercise even when they are in their cage. The minimum size for two birds is 20 by 14 by 14 inches (51 by 36 by 36 cm). Remember that parakeets fly across a cage, rather than up and down, so avoid tall, narrow cages.

Parakeets are sociable birds and like to live in groups.

If possible, also buy a large enclosure called an **indoor flight** so your parakeets have plenty of room to fly. Some of these are collapsible and can be put out of the way when the birds are not using them. The average size is 3 feet wide, 2 feet tall, and 2 feet deep (90 by 60 x 60 cm).

Finding the Right Place
Choose a suitable room for your parakeets.

Parakeets cages are often very handsome and look attractive in any room.

- The cage should be in a room where the parakeets will have plenty of human company, but the room must be made safe so the parakeets can fly free.
- Parakeets hate drafts, so the cage should be placed several feet above the ground. The cage should not be in direct sunlight, or the birds will get too hot.
- Parakeets can be upset by smoke. Avoid putting them near open fires, and if there are smokers in the house, ask them to smoke in another room.

Keet Care
Some bird enthusiasts like to keep more than one type of bird in an aviary. If you keep parakeets, the best companions you could get for them are cockatiels. Parakeets and cockatiels both come from the same part of Australia and eat the same types of foods.

Inside a Cage

A few special pieces of equipment and some toys turn a cage into a comfortable home for your parakeets.

Parakeets appreciate having perches of different widths.

The Essentials

- Line the floor of the cage with a layer of sand or a sheet of sandpaper to catch droppings.
- Attach a water bottle to the inside of the cage.
- Place two pots in the cage — one for seed, and one for **grit**. The pots can be made of clay or stainless steel. Do not place the pots under perches, or the food will be spoiled by keet droppings.

Perches

Perches are the most important feature of a cage or an aviary. Parakeets need a number of perches they can fly to and from. They use perches when they are eating, preening, and sleeping. They also use them to watch activity outside their cages. Parakeets that are good friends will often share a perch.

Most cages come with ready-made perches, but the standard 1/2-inch (12-millimeter), smooth, wooden perch is too narrow for parakeets. Branches from fruit trees, such as apple or pear trees, make excellent perches. Select branches of varying thickness to give your parakeets a choice.

Ladders

Parakeets are great climbers, and they enjoy climbing ladders to reach different levels of their cage. Be sure that the spaces between the rungs of the ladders are not so narrow that a parakeet could trap its head or its body between them.

Playtime

Parakeets are intelligent birds. They need to have things to do, or they will become bored and unhappy. A curious parakeet will investigate every new object in its cage, and toys can provide good entertainment. Change the toys frequently, offering a different toy every day or so, to give your parakeets plenty of variety.

Parakeets are little acrobats and love to climb and swing.

- Bells — Parakeets can learn how to ring bells!
- Swings — Parakeets are good acrobats.
- Mirrors — When a parakeet sees its reflection, it will talk to it as if it were another bird.
- Ping pong balls or empty thread spools on a string — Parakeets can have hours of fun with toys like these.

Keet Care

Parakeets like to peck at their toys, so choose wooden toys rather than plastic ones. Sharp splinters can break off plastic toys when the parakeets gnaw on them.

The Right Choice

Signs of a healthy parakeet

Make sure that the bird you choose is fit and healthy.

Eyes
Look for bright, clear eyes. Dull eyes could mean poor health.

Body
A parakeet should hold its body upright. A hunched back could be a sign that the bird is unwell.

Breathing
Check the parakeet's breathing. It should be rapid but quiet.

Vent
The vent should be clean and dry. A wet, green, dirty vent could mean the bird is sick.

Cere
This patch of skin should be clean and should show no sign of crustiness.

Plumage
Feathers should be sleek and held close to the body. Ragged, untidy feathers show that the bird is in poor condition.

Claws
A parakeets uses its claws to grip a perch. Parakeets with **deformed** claws will not be able to grip properly.

Behavior
A parakeet should appear alert and curious.

If you want an unusual color or kind of parakeet, go to a breeder. Many pet stores now specialize in birds, and the staff will be able to give expert advice. Before you buy a parakeet, look around the store and make sure that the birds for sale are kept in clean conditions and are fit and healthy.

The best time to buy a parakeet is when the bird is six or seven weeks old. Birds are much easier to tame while they are still young. A young parakeet will have black, wavy patterning on its head, reaching down to its cere. These markings disappear when a keet goes through its first **molt**.

Male or Female?

Unless you want to breed parakeets, the best plan is to choose two cocks or two hens. Both can be taught to speak, but males are better talkers than females.

A young hen will have a bluish-white cere, which will turn brown with age. A young cock will have a pinkish-purple cere, which will turn blue.

Keet Care

A parakeet's **throat spots** are a clue to its age. An adult bird will have large, black spots around the front of its throat. Young birds have lots of small spots or flecks of black on their throats.

Note the blue cere and the large throat spots on this cock parakeet.

This hen has a bluish-white cere.

Making Friends

Parakeets become very tame and enjoy spending time with their owners.

For the first few days after bringing your parakeets home, talk to them while they are in their cage. Give them a chance to get to know you.

Hand Training

- As you check the seed pots and the water in their cage, your parakeets will become used to your hand. Take your time so the birds realize your hand is nothing to be afraid of.
- Now hold out your index finger (the finger next to your thumb) like a perch.

In time, the keet will hop onto your finger.

- If your parakeet will not sit on your finger, try holding out a perch or even a pencil.
- When the parakeet seems comfortable perching on your finger, bring it out of its cage. Move slowly so you do not alarm the bird.
- A parakeet does not like to be touched on its back or its tail. If you stroke your pet under its beak and on its chest, it will feel as if it is being preened by another bird and will relax.

Train your parakeets to come to you, either landing on your hand or on a perch.

You will have a lot of fun watching your parakeets enjoy their freedom.

Free Flight

Before you let your parakeets out of their cage, you must make sure the room is safe.

- Close all the doors and windows.
- Be sure that other pets, such as dogs or cats, are out of the room.
- The first time you let your birds out, close the curtains. When a parakeet first explores a room, it may fly into windows, not realizing that glass is solid.

Home Time

Parakeets like to fly free. As long as the rooms are safe and secure, there is no reason they should not spend several hours each day outside their cages. Eventually, you will want to put your birds back in their cage, however, which is why hand training is so important. If your parakeets are used to landing on your finger and staying there, you will be able to carry the birds back to their cage. Have some treats handy so you can give your parakeets rewards when they come to you.

Keet Care

Some house plants, such as poinsettias, are poisonous to parakeets. Just to be safe, remove all houseplants before letting your parakeets out of their cage.

Feeding Time

Parakeets are not fussy eaters, so providing a well-balanced diet is easy.

Seeds, which are what parakeets eat in the wild, are the most important food for pet parakeets. You can buy a seed mix made especially for parakeets, but you should check what the mix contains. Ideally, you want a mix that includes red rape, linseed, or niger seeds along with the more common canary seed and millet.

Your parakeets will need fresh seeds every day.

Green Food

Favorite green foods include grass that is going to seed, dandelion leaves, chickweed, and salad greens. Fresh green foods add variety to a parakeet's diet. You can feed your bird different types of food, as long as you give them only small quantities. Some pet stores sell pots of seed that just need watering to start them growing. You can attach a pot to the bars of the cage, and the grass or green food will grow through the bars.

Keet Care

Parakeets crack seeds open to get to the **kernels**, but they do not eat the outer part of the seed, called the **husk**. Clear away the empty husks every day, or your parakeets will not be able to find the seeds.

Your parakeets will become tamer if you hand-feed them.

Treats

Give your parakeets slices of apples or carrots as treats when you are hand training. Never give your parakeet human foods other than fresh vegetables. Other human foods can be very harmful to birds.

Millet

Parakeets love millet. You can buy branches of millet at most pet stores. Give millet as a treat but do not let your parakeets eat too much millet because it is fattening.

Grit

Parakeets do not have teeth. They swallow seeds whole, and the seeds pass into the bird's **gizzard**. A gizzard is like a grinding machine, but it needs grit, which is like very coarse sand, to work properly. Caged birds need to swallow grit so they can digest their food. Grit is available at pet stores and should always be put in its own pot inside the cage.

Minerals

To provide a well-balanced diet for parakeets, add some extra minerals and iodine. These nutrients can be supplied in a mineral block. A cuttlefish bone attached to the bars of a cage has double value. It contains calcium, and parakeets enjoy pecking at it.

A parakeet cannot resist munching on millet.

Parakeet Care

Find some time every day to make sure your parakeets are happy, clean, and comfortable.

Parakeets cannot clean up after themselves. It is your job to clean their cage and to make sure the birds are in good health.

Daily Tasks

- Check the water bottle and refill if necessary.
- Clear away empty seed husks.
- Remove the sandpaper at the bottom of the cage and replace it with a new sheet.
- Check the free flight area and clean up droppings.

Weekly Tasks

- Take everything out of the cage – toys, ladders, perches, food pots, and water bottle – so you can clean out the cage.
- Wash all the equipment before putting it back in the cage.

Nails and Beaks

Parakeets' nails will wear down naturally if your parakeets have perches that are the correct widths for them to hold onto. Their beaks will also wear down

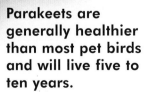

Parakeets are generally healthier than most pet birds and will live five to ten years.

if they have a cuttlefish bone to peck at. Keep a close watch on both nails and beaks, or your parakeets may become very uncomfortable.

If a parakeet's nails are too long, the bird cannot grip a perch. If its beak becomes overgrown, a parakeet will not be able to get the seed kernels out of the husks and will quickly starve. Both nails and beaks can be clipped, but only by a veterinarian or an expert bird keeper.

Molting

Parakeets molt, or shed their feathers, several times a year. The main molt is usually in fall. During the molt, the long tail and flight feathers will fall off and regrow first, followed by the smaller body feathers. You will be surprised at the number of feathers on the cage floor, but parakeets quickly regrow their feathers and look sleek and beautiful again.

Bath Time

Parakeets keep their feathers looking good by preening.

Parakeets produce an oil in a gland in their lower backs. They use the oil to preen their feathers.

A parakeet uses its beak to comb through its feathers, applying oil from the special gland in its rump. In order to preen itself properly, a parakeet needs to wet its feathers. Most parakeets love taking a bath, and it is fun to watch them. Provide a saucer of lukewarm water and sit back to watch your parakeets splash and play.

Keet Care

You can give your parakeet a shower by spraying it with water, using the same kind of bottle that is used for spraying plants.

Trick Training

Parakeets are very clever. When your birds are tame, you can teach them tricks.

All parakeets can learn to perform tricks. You will enjoy training your parakeets, and the birds will like the chance to use their brains. To start, work hard at hand training so your parakeet trusts you and comes to you when you hold out a finger. The more time you spend with your parakeet, handling it and training it, the better it will like you and see you as a special member of its flock.

To get the best effort from your parakeet, keep training sessions to about fifteen minutes. Do not try to train a bird if it is busy feeding or preening, and do not wake it for a training session if it is napping during the day. A sleeping parakeet perches on one leg with its head tucked under its wing.

You can train your parakeet to land on almost any object in a room.

Climbing Ladders

Parakeets climb ladders naturally, so a good trick to start with is getting your parakeet to climb a ladder when you ask it to. Parakeets are good mimics, so all you have to do is use your fingers to "climb up" a ladder. It will not be long before your parakeet copies you, and, as soon as it sees your fingers on a ladder, it will start to climb.

Ringing a Bell

Parakeets love this trick, which is very easy to teach. Simply ring a bell, and wait for your parakeet to copy you. If your parakeet is slow to get the idea, you can let the bird perch on your finger and move it up to the bell. When your parakeet rings the bell, be ready to give it a treat as a reward.

Happy Landings

When your parakeet is used to following your hand, you can teach it to land on different objects. These objects can be anything from a toy car to a bowl of fruit or even the top of your head!

Keet Care

If you want your parakeet to have a very special reward, you can give it a tiny dab of honey. Parakeets love this sweet treat, but you should give them only small amounts or your birds will gain too much weight.

When your parakeet learns to trust you, it will treat you as a special friend and will want you to join in its playtime.

Talking Parakeets

Parakeets imitate human voices when they do not have bird sounds to copy.

You can teach most parakeets to say a few words or to copy tunes or household noises. Cocks are easier to teach than hens, but, with patience, you can train either one to talk to you.

First Lessons

- Start with an easy word, such as your pet's name, as long as it is an easy name like Joey, rather than a difficult one such as Alexander.
- Use a high-pitched voice as you say the name.
- Keep repeating the name and reward any attempt your bird makes to copy you.
- Be patient. It may take time before your pet catches on.

Some parakeets learn to repeat whole sentences. Others become expert at copying songs or sounds, such as a phone ringing or a dog barking.

Teaching your parakeet to talk is fun, but you also need to listen to your parakeet so you understand how it is feeling.

Parakeets are alert, intelligent birds. Many keets learn to mimic words and sounds.

Happy Parakeets

A contented parakeet will sit proudly on its perch, chattering or warbling quietly. Happy parakeets like to sing along to music, too, and you may hear them warbling if you leave a radio on. A happy parakeet will also grind its beak as if it is cracking seeds.

Alert Parakeets

An alert parakeet is interested in everything that goes on. A cheerful cry of "backpack ack," often accompanied by bobbing, means "Take a look at this!"

Frightened Parakeets

A frightened parakeet will perch with its feathers flattened and its eyes alert, ready to take off at any second.

Unhappy Parakeets

An unhappy parakeet will hold its wings away from its body and pant with its beak open. It may close its eyes for brief periods and call out a high-pitched "fweep." A parakeet showing this behavior may be ill, scared, or simply too warm. Seek expert help if your parakeet seems unhappy.

Angry Parakeets

A parakeet is rarely aggressive, but if it is handled roughly, it will cry out "ark, ark, ark" and may even bite.

A parakeet often feeds its companion as a special sign of affection.

Glossary

Aborigines: the original peoples of Australia

allergy: a reaction to certain substances, such as the fur of animals, that results in health problems

aviaries: large enclosures for keeping birds

cere: the waxy skin above a parakeet's nose

chicks: baby parakeets

cocks: male parakeets

contour feathers: small, curved feathers that cover a bird's body

deformed: unnatural in shape

drought: a long period with no rainfall

fledge: to fly and leave the nest

flight feathers: long feathers at the ends of the wings

flocks: large groups of birds

gizzard: part of a bird's digestive system, used for grinding seeds

grit: small, sharp stones

hens: female parakeets

husk: the outer covering of a seed

indoor flight: an indoor enclosure big enough for birds to fly in

kernels: innermost part of seeds

mimics: animals that imitate others

molt: the process of shedding feathers and growing new ones

naturalist: a person who studies the natural world

outback: the remote areas of Australia

pied: having patches of color

plumage: the feathers that cover a bird's body

preening: cleaning and arranging feathers

streamlined: having a smooth, sleek shape

throat spots: black spots or flecks at the front of a parakeet's throat

More Books to Read

101 Facts About Parakeets
101 Facts About Pets (series)
Julia Barnes
(Gareth Stevens)

Parakeets
Junior Pet Care (series)
Zuza Vrbova
(Chelsea House)

Parakeets
Pet Care (series)
Kelley MacAuley &
Bobbie Kalman
(Crabtree)

Taking Care of Your Parakeet
Young Pet Owner's Guides
(series)
Helen Piers
(Barron's Educational)

Web Sites

Budgie Madness
www.geocities.com/Heartland/3749/index.html

Budgie Varieties
www.parrotparrot.com/budgies/

How to Buy, Raise, and Train a Parakeet
www.lisashea.com/petinfo/budgie.html

Note to educators and parents: The publisher has carefully reviewed these Web sites to ensure that they are suitable for children. Many Web sites change frequently, however, and Gareth Stevens, Inc., cannot guarantee that a site's future contents will continue to meet our high standards of quality and educational value. Be advised that children should be closely supervised whenever they access the Internet.

Index